T0358095

The Gingerbread Man

Retold and dramatised as a reading play
for partners or small groups.

Ellie Hallett

Ways to read this story

This story is suitable for school and home. Some 'how to read' ideas are below.

- With a partner or small group, take it in turns to read the rows.

- Don't rush! This helps you to say each word clearly.

- Think of yourselves as actors by adding lots of facial and vocal expression. Small gaps of silence also create dramatic energy. These techniques will bring the story to life.

- If you meet a new word, try to break it down and then say it again. If you have any problems, ask your teacher or a reading buddy.

- Don't be scared of unusual words. They will become your new best friends.
  (New words strengthen your general knowledge and enable you to become vocabulary-rich in your day-to-day life.)

Have fun!

'I think I'll do some baking today and make a gingerbread man.'

'What a good idea, dear wife. But how will you do that?'

'First I'll mix the ingredients for the gingerbread dough, and then I'll shape it into a smart little man.'

'He already sounds delicious!'

'And then, dear husband, I'll add a few finishing touches before popping him into the oven.'

'You are a very clever cook, dear wife. And a gingerbread man will be perfect for our morning tea!'

'He certainly will! I think he's going to be a tasty little champion.'

Fifteen minutes later

'And out of the oven he comes. I'll rest him here on the windowsill so that he can cool down.'

'I'll put the kettle on to make us a big pot of tea, dear wife.'

'Oh my goodness! Our dear little gingerbread man is escaping!'

'Escaping? But he is not a real ...'

'I can't believe what I'm seeing! He has jumped over the flower garden, and now he's off down the road!'

'Stop, stop, little Gingerbread Man! We want to have you for our morning tea.'

'Ha ha ha! Hee hee hee!
You can't catch me for your morning tea!
I can run very fast, I can, I can,
And that's because I'm the Gingerbread Man!'

'I've run away from a little old woman and a little old man, but you can't catch me, I'm the Gingerbread Man.'

'But what's this? A large dog with a noisy bark is now running after me.'

'Woof, woof!

Stop, stop, little Gingerbread Man!

I want to have you for morning tea.'

'Ha ha ha! Hee hee hee!

You can't catch me for your morning tea!

I can run very fast, I can, I can,

And that's because I'm the Gingerbread Man!'

'I've run away from a little old woman and a little old man, so I can run away from you, I can!'

'But what's this?

A jolly pink pig has joined the race!'

'Oink, oink!

Stop, stop, little Gingerbread Man!

I want to have you for morning tea!'

'Ha ha ha! Hee hee hee!

You can't catch me for your morning tea!

I can run very fast, I can, I can,

And that's because I'm the Gingerbread Man!'

'I've run away from a barking dog, a little old woman and a little old man, so I can run away from you, I can!'

'But what's this?

A dairy cow with a bell around her neck has her eye on me!

Surely a cow doesn't like gingerbread!'

'Moo, moo!

Stop, stop, little Gingerbread Man!

I want to have you for morning tea!'

'Ha ha ha! Hee hee hee!

You can't catch me for your morning tea!

I can run very fast, I can, I can,

And that's because I'm the Gingerbread Man!'

'I've run away from a jolly pink pig, a barking dog, a little old woman and a little old man, so I can run away from you, I can!'

'But what's this?

A lanky farm worker with long legs is running after me!

Surely he is too busy to eat gingerbread!'

'Whatever is that? Oh **yes!**

Stop, stop little Gingerbread Man.

I want to share you with the boys
for morning tea!'

'Ha ha ha! Hee hee hee!

You can't catch me for your morning tea!

I can run very fast, I can, I can,

And that's because I'm the Gingerbread Man!'

'I've run away from a dairy cow, a jolly pink pig, a barking dog, a little old woman and a little old man, so I can run away from you, I can!'

'But what's this?

A galloping horse has joined the chase!

Surely a horse doesn't like gingerbread!'

'Neigh! Neigh!
Stop, stop, little Gingerbread Man!
I want to have you for morning tea!'

'Ha ha ha! Hee hee hee!

You can't catch me for your morning tea!

I can run very fast, I can, I can,

And that's because I'm the Gingerbread Man!'

'I've run away from a lanky farm worker, a dairy cow, a jolly pink pig, a barking dog, a little old woman and a little old man, so I can run away from you, I can!'

'But what's this?

The road stops at a river.

No matter. There's sure to be a boat around here somewhere!'

'Why hello there. I'm called Fox, and you seem to be in a mighty big hurry.

Is anything the matter?'

'I'm the Gingerbread Man, and I've run away from a galloping horse, a lanky farm worker, a dairy cow, a jolly pink pig, a barking dog, a little old woman and a little old man.
They want to eat me for their morning tea.'

'This could be your lucky day, sweet little Gingerbread Man.
I am particularly good at helping those in need of assistance, especially in an emergency.'

'This certainly is an emergency, Mr Fox.
But how are you able to help me?'

'I am about to cross the river, so if you care to jump up onto my tail, we'll be off.'

'And in case you are worried, I don't usually eat between meals.'

'Please do not concern yourself that you are in any danger at this point in time, dear friend.'

'Oh thank you, thank you, Mr Fox.'

'I like to have a swim on a warm summer morning. Please sit back and enjoy your river cruise.'

'Excuse me, Mr Fox! Ahem ... I hate to mention this, but I'm getting rather wet here on your tail.'

'May I, um, perhaps climb up onto your back?'

'Sincere apologies for neglecting my duties, Mr Gingerbread.'

'Please be my guest! Hop up onto the comfort of my back so that you stay high and dry.'

'Oh me, oh my, Ginger, old pal. We seem to have a loading problem.'

'You, I'm afraid, have become rather heavy on my back.'

'Could you possibly hop up onto my nose? It will help me to keep my balance in this strong river current.'

'Not at all. Not at all! And may I say how well you swim, Mr Fox!'

'Why, thank you! The pleasure is all mine. You are more than welcome.'

'Well, here we are at the shore, so you may now disembark.'

'I'm especially glad that you have remained dry and crisp.'

'Crisp, Mr Fox? Why is crisp important?'

'A gingerbread man is made to be eaten, and you are absolutely perfect as a mid-morning snack.

Ah yes! Delicious.'

And that, I'm afraid, was that!

The Readers' Theatre series by Ellie Hallett

These **Readers' Theatre** stories have a major advantage in that everyone has equal reading time. Best of all, they are theatrical, immediately engaging and entertaining. Ellie Hallett's unique play-in-rows format, developed and trialled with great success in her own classrooms, combines expressive oral reading, active listening, peer teaching, vocabulary building, visualisation, and best of all, enjoyment.

ISBN	Title	Author	Price	E-book Price	QTY
9781921016455	Goldilocks and The Three Bears	Hallett, Ellie	9.95	9.95	
9781925398045	Jack and the Beanstalk	Hallett, Ellie	9.95	9.95	
9781925398069	The Fox and the Goat	Hallett, Ellie	9.95	9.95	
9781925398076	The Gingerbread Man	Hallett, Ellie	9.95	9.95	
9781925398052	Little Red Riding Hood and the Five Senses	Hallett, Ellie	9.95	9.95	
9781925398083	The Town Mouse and the Country Mouse	Hallett, Ellie	9.95	9.95	
9781925398014	The Two Travellers	Hallett, Ellie	9.95	9.95	
9781925398007	The Enormous Turnip	Hallett, Ellie	9.95	9.95	
9781925398090	The Hare and the Tortoise	Hallett, Ellie	9.95	9.95	
9781925398106	The Wind and the Sun	Hallett, Ellie	9.95	9.95	
9781925398113	The Three Wishes	Hallett, Ellie	9.95	9.95	
9781921016554	The Man, the Boy and the Donkey	Hallett, Ellie	9.95	9.95	
9781925398120	The Fox and the Crow	Hallett, Ellie	9.95	9.95	
9781920824921	Who Will Bell the Cat?	Hallett, Ellie	9.95	9.95	
9781925398021	The Ugly Duckling	Hallett, Ellie	9.95	9.95	

KNOWLEDGE
BOOKS and SOFTWARE

PUBLISHING

www.kbs.com.au

Readers' Theatre